SCOTTIE BOOKS

EXPLORING SCOTTISH SEASHORES

By John Baxter
Illustrated by Fhiona Galloway

Edinburgh : HMSO
Scottish Natural Heritage
National Museums of Scotland

SEASHORES OF SCOTLAND

The coastline of Scotland is over 11,800 km long. This is more than the distance of a return trip between Glasgow and New York!

Around Scotland there are high rock cliffs plunging steeply into the sea – for example on Fair Isle. Flat rocky shores with boulders and pebbles can be found near Dunbar and in parts of many of the sealochs of western Scotland. In other places there are long inviting stretches of sand as at St Cyrus and in the Solway Firth. In the large estuaries such as the Firth of Forth and the Firth of Clyde there are great expanses of mud.

OUTER HEBRIDES

SKYE

F

BA
RO

SOLWAY FIRTH

SHETLAND ISLANDS

ORKNEY ISLANDS

FAIR ISLE

MORAY FIRTH

OF FORTH

Shores exposed to the full force of the wind are lashed by gales and battered by waves. Only a few animals and plants can survive on them. Shores like this can be found on the Orkney and Shetland Islands, Fair Isle and St Kilda, and also on mainland Scotland. A greater variety of animals and plants can be seen on more sheltered shores, for instance the bays, inlets and sealochs on the west coast and parts of the east coast.

All these different types of seashores are worth exploring. It is exciting to make notes on what you find living there and to compare one shore with another.

WHAT ARE SEASHORES?

So how would **you** describe the seashore? The seashore can be all of the following:

The place where the land and the sea meet. It is covered and uncovered by the sea twice every 24 hours when the tide comes in and goes out.

It is a place to go to collect food, such as snails and crabs and even seaweed. This still happens in Scotland, particularly on the islands. It is a place to go to relax, sunbathe and swim. However, it is often too cold to do these in Scotland. See if you can find out how sunny and warm it is at a beach near you either by taking your own records or looking them up in the local paper.

The seashore is a wonderful place to go to discover many different animals and plants, from the tiniest worms and delicate sea anemones to birds and seals. It is also a place to explore, where you can find many different species of animals and plants and strange and interesting things which have been washed up by the waves: flotsam and jetsam. Do you know the difference? It is interesting to search along the strand line, which is the line of 'rubbish' just above high tide mark, to see what has been washed ashore, but take care as some may be dangerous.

Make a list of all the different objects you find. Then try to say where each came from.

Did You Know?

The movement of the tide is caused by the pull of the sun and the moon. When they are in line (either when the moon is full or new) the tides go out and come in further than when they are at right angles to each other (when the moon is crescent shaped).

ROCK, SAND AND MUD

The seashore is usually made of rock, sand or mud. There may be bits of all three on the shore you visit.

On rocky shores the animals and plants can be found living on the surface of the rocks or in cracks and crevices. These rocks may be on sand or gravel. You might find other animals living buried in the sand. All these different places are worth exploring. Some animals and plants may even be growing on other animals or plants.

Spiral wrack

Bladder wrack

Serrated wrack

Kelp

In some places the seashore has been replaced by piers and jetties or buildings made by humans. In most cases these will also have animals and plants growing on them.

Make a map of part of the coast near where you live. Try to show the different types of shores and any man-made structures which have been built there. Keep lists of the different animals and plants you find there. Were they living on rock or in sand or mud?

Oyster catcher

On sandy and muddy shores there are far fewer plants to be seen. Most of the animals live buried in the sand or mud. Usually there is no sign of what is beneath the surface and you have to dig to find out. In some cases the animal will leave tell-tale signs on the surface. See if you can find any of these signs and discover what is making them.

Tellin

Spoot

Sea potato

Lugworm

LIVING ON THE SEASHORE

Animals and plants have developed in different ways to help them survive on the shore. Because they constantly get hit by waves they have to hold on to the rock or escape by hiding somewhere.

Worms Many worms living on sandy or muddy shores build tubes below the surface of the sand. Here they can escape the effects of the waves.

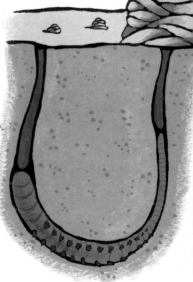

Snails Many species of snail crawl into crevices to escape the worst of the action of the waves.

Limpets have a large sucker-like foot. Limpets clamp down on rocks using this foot. It also lets them move about when the waves are not too strong.

Barnacles cement their shells onto the rock.

Seaweed holdfast Although this looks something like the roots of plants found on land it is only intended to attach the seaweed to the rock. It does not take up food or water as the roots of plants on land do.

Sea anemones catch their prey with 'poisoned darts'.

Limpets scrape tiny plants off the surface of the rocks.

Cockles draw in water. Water contains microscopic animals and plants which the cockle then filters out for food.

Starfish dissolve barnacles out of their shells.

Barnacles lie on their backs inside their shells. They wave their legs to draw water and food to their mouths.

Seabirds use their beaks to probe the sand and mud for shells.

Tellins 'hoover' the surface of the sand picking up microscopic organisms.

Spoots Like a number of other shellfish, the razor shell or spoot is able to burrow deep into the sand to escape the effects of the waves.

How do you think the animals and plants you find on the seashore manage to survive? Remember different animals have developed different ways of feeding.

9

ROCKPOOLS

Many of the rocky shores around Scotland have rockpools. Some are shallow, some are deep, some are large and some are small. Here you can see in miniature what the shore looks like when the tide is in.

Rockpool-watching can be fun, especially if you have a goggle box. Find a rockpool which is not too deep and which maybe has some stones on the bottom. Sit or stand quietly beside it for a few minutes. Take care that your shadow does not fall over the rockpool. You will see the seaweeds all standing up as if the tide is in. But more exciting are the animals such as limpets, winkles, crabs, shrimps and small fish, all moving around. Make a drawing of what you see. Make a list of all the animals and plants in the rockpool. Then compare this list with those you find on the rock around the rockpool.

How to make a Gogglebox!

1. Find a strong plastic container and clean it out.

2. Cut off both ends and sand down the sharp edges.

3. Put a clear plastic bag round one end and secure with an elastic band.

If you can't find a rockpool why not make your own? Fill a plastic bucket with salt water and keep it in a shady place so that the water does not warm up too quickly. Collect a few different animals which you find on the shore. Place these in the bucket and then wait and watch. Make notes of what happens once you put the animals into your rockpool. When you are finished make sure you return the animals and stones to the place from which you collected them.

SPOT THE DIFFERENCE

The animals and plants on the shore can survive when the tide is in and when it is out but there are differences in what they do, how they appear and where they are found. There are 8 differences in these pictures. See how many you can spot. *(Answers on page 40.)*

13

SEAWEEDS

Seaweeds are the main group of plants which can be found on the shores of Scotland.

Seaweeds do not have roots but instead have a holdfast. The holdfast fixes the seaweeds to the rock. However it does not absorb water or food as proper roots do. The stem of seaweeds is known as the 'stipe' and at the end of this, or branching off it, are leaf-like 'fronds'.

Seaweeds come in many different shapes, sizes and colours. There are:

Green seaweeds
Brown seaweeds
Red seaweeds

See how many different species of these different coloured seaweeds you can find.

The largest and most obvious seaweeds on the shore are the brown seaweeds. Different species of brown seaweeds are found in bands at different levels on the shore. If you can identify a small number of seaweeds you can always tell where you are on the shore. Many different animals eat seaweeds, others hide amongst the fronds (or leaves) or live attached to it.

Some seaweeds are eaten by humans, such as the red seaweeds dulse and laver.

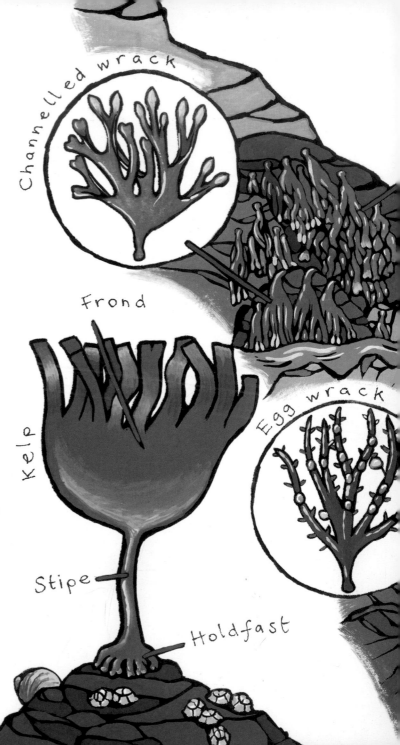

Channelled wrack

Frond

Egg wrack

Kelp

Stipe

Holdfast

Spiral wrack

Bladder wrack

Serrated wrack

Did you know

Seaweeds are used to help make lots of things. For example, ice-cream, jelly, toothpaste, beer, dyes (and many more).

Tooth Paste

DYE

SPONGES AND SEA ANEMONES

Sponges

Sponges are made up of tiny animals living together in colonies.

You can search for sponges under stones and pebbles in rockpools or on the underside of overhanging rock ledges where it is damp and shaded from direct sunlight. They can be found on nearly all rocky shores in Scotland.

The breadcrumb sponge is the most common sponge found on the shore. It is flat and can be found in various colours but most commonly green or orange. On its surface the breadcrumb sponge has a number of large holes which look like miniature volcanoes. The sponge draws in water through these holes which it filters for minute food particles and oxygen. This water is then pushed out through more numerous but much smaller holes, which are much more difficult to see. Try drawing a piece of sponge and count the numbers of large holes and small holes.

The sponges you find on the shores of Scotland are related to the large sponges which were used in the bath and which live in warmer waters in the tropics. Too many of these have been collected and now most bath sponges are man-made.

Breadcrumb Sponge

Purse Sponge

Sea Anemones

Sea anemones are animals! They are called anemones because they look like an open flower. The 'petals' of the 'flower' are tentacles with which the sea anemone captures small pieces of food. They capture food by firing tiny poisoned darts on a thread. They then pull their prey in to their mouths using their tentacles.

The beadlet anemone is the most common sea anemone on the shore, and it is found all around Scotland. It is usually red or green with a ring of blue dots at the base of the tentacles. It lives attached to rocks. The tentacles are very sensitive and can be drawn back very quickly when touched. This is so that the anemone can stop small fish nipping off its tentacles. You can see this by lightly touching the tentacles. See how long it is before the tentacles reappear. Repeat this a number of times. What do you find?

The green snakelocks anemone has very long tentacles which unlike the beadlet anemone cannot be drawn back when touched. Watch out! The tentacles have a lot of poison darts, and a sting can be painful.

Snakelocks Anemones

Beadlet Anemones

WORMS

Worms are very common animals on Scottish seashores. There are many different species which come in many different shapes and sizes. Some worms eat by filtering tiny animals and plants out of the seawater, others eat dead and decaying material and some feed on the bacteria and other microscopic life living in the sand. Worms in turn are eaten by many different animals, especially fish and birds.

Lugworms live in a U-shaped burrow, buried in the sand with a hole at one end of the burrow and a mound of coiled sand at the other end. The coiled sand on the shore is the only sign of this worm. Fishermen like to use lugworms as bait.

Ragworms live buried in the sand. They leave no sign of themselves on the surface. You will need to dig in the sand to try to find ragworms. They are the favourite bait of fishermen.

Keel worms and spiral worms are closely related species that live in chalky tubes which they make and cement to the rock surface or the fronds of seaweed. The worms stay in the tube for protection and only stick out their head of tentacles to catch food particles passing in the water.

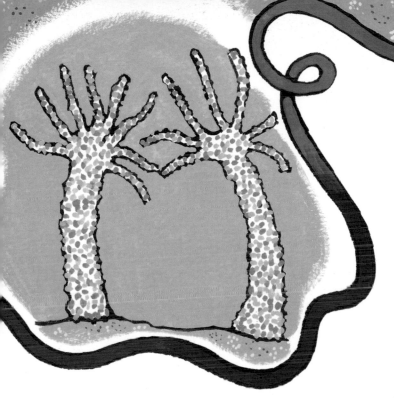

Sandmason worms build fragile tubes made out of sand grains. The distinctive tubes stick out of the sand by a few centimetres but if they are carefully dug out of the sand, you can see they are much longer.

Scale worms are fast-moving worms which live under stones or on seaweed. They are often brightly coloured and patterned and if you catch them they shed their scales as they try to escape.

Bootlace worms are very long worms – they can reach up to at least 5 metres in length. You can find them in muddy gravel underneath stones on the shore.

Can you identify these different worms? (Answers on page 40.) How many of these or other worms can you find on the shore?

A Seashore Adventure

Make a counter from a piece of cardboard.
Draw your own seashore animal or plant on it.

You have forgotten your gogglebox, go back to the start!

High tide, miss a turn.

You take some time at the rockpool, miss a turn.

You have left the rocks turned over, miss 2 turns.

The tide has turned, go back 4 places.

Start

LIMPETS

A limpet is a mollusc with a cone-shaped shell.

You can find limpets on most rocky shores around Scotland. Sometimes there are lots of them.

A limpet can clamp down very tightly on to the rock using its large, muscular foot. This ensures it does not get knocked off by the waves even in the stormiest conditions. When the tide is out, its large foot makes a seal to make sure that it does not dry out.

Do you think you are stronger than a limpet? Find a limpet on the open rock. Try to push it off with your finger. It may move very slightly at first but it will quickly clamp down hard and refuse to budge. Try again on a limpet living in a rock pool or a very damp place, maybe under seaweed. You may be able to remove it, if you are very quick, or it may just move a little before it clamps down like the one on the open rock.

Tortoiseshell limpet

Blue-rayed limpet

22

Limpets move about over the rock feeding by using their long, hard, file-like tongues to scrape tiny plants off the rock. You can often see the feeding trails of limpets as a zig-zag pattern on the rock. See if you can find these feeding trails. After feeding, each limpet will return to the place on the rock from where it set out. A limpet can live for many years and it always returns to the same point. Over the years it makes an oval mark on the rock known as a 'home scar'. Try to find these marks on the rock which are left vacant as a result of limpets dying.

SNAILS

Snails are also molluscs but with spiral shells which come in many shapes, sizes and colours:

Winkles – includes these three species (edible, rough, flat)

Rough winkle

Edible winkle

Flat winkle

Painted topshell

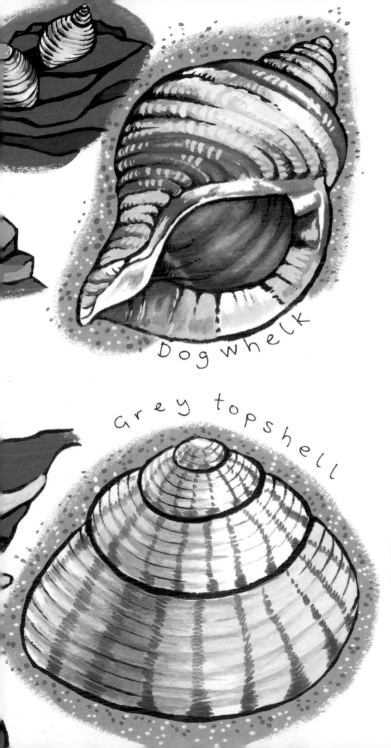

Dog whelk

Grey topshell

Many different species of snail are found on Scottish shores. See how many kinds you can find on a rocky shore and compare these to those you can find on a sandy or muddy shore. On rocky shores you will find some in cracks in the rock, some under boulders or in rockpools and others on seaweed. Can you tell which species prefer to live where? Make drawings of the different shell shapes and the different patterns.

When you pick up a shell with a snail inside, it hides by drawing itself into the shell, closing the entrance with a horny plate. To see snails moving about you can either sit quietly and watch them in a rockpool or put some in a clear plastic container full of sea water. If left alone they will come out of their shells and begin to move about. If you look up from the underside of the container you should see the large muscular foot which the snail uses to glide over the rock on a sticky trail of mucus. Old snail trails can sometimes be seen on the rock.

Small grains of sand get stuck on the rock leaving the images of these winding trails. See if you can find any snail trails and draw them.

CRABS

Hunting for crabs can be exciting. When the tide is out most crabs tend to hide under seaweed or stones and you can get a surprise when you find them.

There are three common species of crabs found on Scottish shores. If it is picked up the green or shore crab will wave its pincers about in attack. The edible crab is generally a reddish-pink colour with black tips to its pincers. It just tucks its pincers in when handled. The hermit crab is the third most common. Make drawings of these crabs and any others you find.

Hermit crab

Shore crab

Most crabs could give you a small nip if handled wrongly. But, with a little care, they can be picked up safely and looked at before being carefully returned. If held this way, the crab can't turn its pincers round to nip you.

The hermit crab uses the empty shells of dead snails to live in. You can often see what seem to be snails moving quickly over the bottom of rockpools. If you look more closely, these shells are actually inhabited by hermit crabs. If you are lucky you might find one looking for a new home. The crab picks up empty shells and turns them round in its pincers before choosing a suitable new shell. It will dart out of one shell and into the other.

All crabs have a soft body protected by a hard shell. At first the shell is soft. Before it hardens the crab makes itself as large as possible. This is so that when the shell hardens, it is larger than the body inside. This gives the crab room to grow. Once it fills this shell it has to cast it off and grow a new one. How many empty crab shells can you find on the shore?

Edible crab

All crabs are scavengers; that is, they feed on dead and rotting material. In this way they help to keep the shore clean.

Spiny-skinned Animals

The echinoderms – or spiny-skinned animals – are a group of animals which are only found in the sea. The best-known echinoderms are starfish and sea urchins. These can be found on most rocky shores in Scotland. Others, such as feather stars and sea cucumbers, are less common but you may be lucky enough to find them near the water's edge.

The upper surface of starfish and sea urchins is rough to touch and covered by spines of different lengths. The body is divided into five segments. In the starfish these are seen as 'arms'. They move around using many hundreds of tiny, sucker-like, tube feet which clamp down and then let go. Put a starfish in a clear plastic container of sea water and watch the action of the tube feet as the animal moves. Try to draw the actions of the tube feet which help the starfish to move.

Starfish

Sea urchins

Feather star

If you want to find a starfish the best place to search is in rockpools or under stones. At certain times of the year you may find very large numbers of tiny starfish which have recently hatched from eggs.

You can usually only find sea urchins very near the water's edge at low tide although they are sometimes found in rockpools higher up. You can often find the empty shell of a sea urchin which has lost all the spines. These are nice to collect but if you take one home make sure it is completely empty as the flesh can smell. It is also best to lightly varnish the surface and keep it out of direct sunlight otherwise the colours will fade very quickly.

Starfish have a mouth on their under surface. They feed by sitting over their prey and dissolving it before sucking it up. Sea urchins eat young kelp plants and other organisms living on the rock surface in shallow water.

SEASHORE FISH

There are many species of fish in the sea around Scotland. How many can you find for sale in your local fishmonger? How do you think they were caught?

Some species of fish prefer living in the shallow waters which cover the shore areas when the tide is in. When the tide goes out they either hide in rockpools or lie under stones where there is enough water trapped to keep them damp until the tide comes back in.

Shores with rockpools or lots of boulders are the best places to hunt for fish and are found all around Scotland. The commonest fish found on the shore are the eelpout and butterfish. These are often found hiding under stones or dense seaweed when the tide is out. When they are uncovered they are able to wriggle away very quickly and are difficult to catch without a net.

Fish which can be found in rockpools when the tide is out include the shanny and the 15-spined stickleback.

15-spined Stickleback

Shanny

Butterfish

Eelpout

More rarely other species of fish, which have been trapped as the tide goes out, are found stranded and dead or in rockpools. You may even find species like the scorpion fish or the lumpsucker.

You can also find some species of fish on sandy shores, particularly around low water mark. If you walk through the shallow water here you may disturb flat fish such as flounders and plaice. Sandeels may also be found here – they are particularly important as food to many species of seabird.

Sandeels

Scorpion fish

Lumpsucker

Plaice

Flounder

SEALS, OTTERS, WHALES AND DOLPHINS

Around the coast of Scotland there are beaches and sandbanks where you can see seals basking in the sun. If you get too close they will move into the water but they will stay and watch you from a safe distance.

There are two species of seals found around Scotland, the more numerous and larger grey seal and the smaller common seal. Apart from the difference in size the two seals can be distinguished by the shape of their heads.

Seals eat fish and in some areas they are in competition with fishermen who think the seals are eating the fish they should be catching. Seals are also accidentally caught in fishing nets and drowned.

Grey

Common

Common Seal

Grey Seal

If you are lucky you might also see otters on the shore, but for this you have to be patient and know where to watch. Otters are shy animals but can be seen on rocky shores playing in the seaweed and feeding on small fish. They are strong swimmers with webbed feet and have sharp claws and teeth for catching and eating their prey. The best place to see otters is on the shores around Shetland and Orkney or in some of the more sheltered sealochs on the west coast of Scotland.

Bottlenose dolphins are not animals of the seashore but, especially around the Moray Firth, you have a good chance of seeing these wonderful creatures swimming and jumping out of the water. Other species of whale and porpoise can be seen off the Scottish coast, or washed up dead or stranded on a beach. Take care, do not approach dead animals as they can be very smelly and may even carry disease.

SHOREBIRDS

Puffin

Razorbill

Guillemot

Many species of birds can be found around the coast of Scotland. Some birds come to breed during the summer. Others, like the waders visit to spend the winter feeding. Some birds, such as gulls, can be seen the whole year round.

Whenever you visit the shore it is always worth taking a pair of binoculars so that you can more closely observe the birds nesting on the cliffs, sitting on the water or feeding on the mudflats.

The auk family includes the puffin which nests in burrows. Its close relatives the guillemot and the razorbill nest on cliff ledges at sites such as the Bass Rock, and in Orkney and Shetland. These birds all have very short wings and can 'fly' under water at great speed as they chase and catch small fish such as sandeels.

Many of the birds which come to the shores of

Scotland for the winter are waders. These birds feed on the worms and molluscs found in the sand and mudflats of estuaries and other large sheltered bays.

The different species of waders feed on different species of worm or mollusc and have specially shaped beaks to help them capture their prey. The curlew has a long curved beak which helps it probe for deep-living worms, while the redshank has a much shorter, straight beak which lets it catch small snails and shrimps. The oystercatcher feeds on shellfish such as cockles, mussels and tellins. It finds these by probing in the sand. Once it has found them, it opens them by smashing them against a rock or prizing them open with its beak.

When visiting a shore, find as many different species of prey as you can, and then decide what birds you might see feeding on them.

Find a good sandy or muddy shore near where you live and visit it regularly over a year. Make a record of the numbers and species of birds present at different times of the year. Compare this list with one for a rocky shore or cliff.

Redshank

Oystercatcher

Curlew

SEAWEED PRESSING AND SHELL ORNAMENTS

Many of the small green and red seaweeds found either growing or washed-up on the shores of Scotland are very fragile and delicate. They can make beautiful patterns when pressed and dried. You can make a collection of the various weeds you find, or, when you become more expert, you can make whole pictures using a combination of seaweeds of different shades and forms.

If you collect seaweed for pressing, take only as much as you think you will need and keep it moist until you get home. Some of the more beautiful and fragile species live in deeper water but may be washed up after a storm. Search the strand line as soon as you can after a storm for any unusual examples. Seaweed does not last long after it has been collected so you will have to press it as soon as possible. You will need a flat-bottomed tray, some water, a paintbrush and some paper, gauze and some old newspaper together with a heavy weight.

Make your own Seaweed Pressings!

1. Fill tray with water, put in the paper then the seaweed.

2. Using a paintbrush spread out the fronds. Drain away the water.

3. Cover the picture with gauze then press between the newspapers and use a weight.

4. Leave for a week then frame!

On any visit to the shore you can always find large numbers of empty shells of different colours and various shapes and sizes. You can collect these, taking care that none are occupied by snails or hermit crabs. They can then be used to make attractive ornaments.

CHANGES TO THE SEASHORE

Although much of the seashore around Scotland can still be seen in its natural beauty, most of it has been changed by humans in one way or another.

GOVERNMENT
WARNING
NO BATHING!

WARNI
DO NO
COLLEC
SHELLFI
FROM BEA

OIL

Developments include docks, power stations, bridges, oil terminals, marinas. How many of these can you find on a piece of coast near you? How many others can you find? All of these have changed the natural seashore.

Many human activities result in pollution, which affects the animals and plants living on the seashore. Pollution can come from sources such as sewers, factories, ships, fish farms and caravan sites. How many different sources of pollution are there affecting the piece of coast near you?

Pollution can be found in many different forms: oil, chemicals sewage, pesticides, litter, for example.

TOXIC

PLACES TO VISIT AND ANSWERS

- St Abbs voluntary marine nature reserve
- Deep Sea World – South Queensferry
- Sealife Centre – St Andrews
             – Oban
- Royal Museum of Scotland
- Isle of May National Nature Reserve
- Moray Firth – Dolphin watching
- Scottish Fishing Museum – Anstruther

Page 4/5
Flotsam is wreckage floated ashore and jetsam is objects thrown overboard.

Page 12/13:
1. Seaweed standing up (tide in) or seaweed lying on the rock (tide out).

2. Birds in flight or sitting on the water surface (tide in) or birds on the shore feeding on limpets etc (tide out).

3. Fish in the water column amongst the seaweed (tide in) or no fish in sight (tide out).

4. Anemones on rock surface with tentacles extended feeding (tide in) or anemones 'closed up' with tentacles withdrawn (tide out).

5. Limpets moving over the rock with shells raised and home scars vacant (tide in) or limpets clamped down tightly on home scars (tide out).

6. Barnacles feeding (tide in) or barnacles closed up and not feeding (tide out).

7. Winkles out on rock and on the surfaces of seaweeds with tentacles etc showing (tide in) winkles either hiding under seaweed or in crevices, in both cases with their heads withdrawn and shells sealed (tide out).

8. Crab out and scavenging (tide in) or crab hiding under stone (tide out).

Page 18/19:
Page 18: bottom left: lugworm
Page 18: top right: keel worms and spiral worms
Page 19: top left: sandmason worms
Page 19: bottom left: scale worms
Page 19: bottom right: rag worm
Pages 18 and 19: around edge: bootlace worm

40

Printed in Scotland for HMSO by CC No. 70343, Dd 293068, C50, 9/95